KU-113-102

THE USBORNE BOOK OF ORIGAMI

Kate Needham

Editor: Cheryl Evans

Origami consultant:
Sarah Goodall

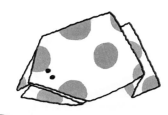

Designed by Carol Law

Illustrated by Angie Sage

Additional ideas by
Ray Gibson

With special thanks to: Wendy Ball,
Debbie Collins, Marissa Goodman,
John Humphrey, Matthew Jones,
Hannah Mander, David Milligan,
Laura Parsons and John Stapleton.

Contents

First published in 1991. This edition 1992. Usborne
Publishing Ltd, Usborne House, 83-85 Saffron Hill,
London EC1N 8RT, England. Copyright © 1992,
1991. Usborne Publishing Ltd.

What is origami?

'Origami' is a Japanese word which means 'paper folding'. Hundreds of years ago, when paper was first invented, the Japanese folded it into dolls and flowers for special ceremonies. Now that paper is cheap and plentiful lots of people fold paper just for fun.

This book teaches you how to make lots of origami toys and decorations. It starts off with simple models and gets harder as you go along. Make sure you start at the beginning. Models marked ☆are the easy ones; models marked ☆☆☆ are the hardest. The tips on these pages will help you before you start.

What sort of paper?

Any paper that folds well is good for origami. Traditional origami paper is coloured on one side. Models are invented so that some bits are white and other bits are coloured.

You can buy packs of coloured squares from good toy departments and Japanese shops. Or you can order them from the British Origami Society (see page 32 for the address).

Useful types of paper

Wrapping paper is good because it has a plain and a coloured side.

Tissue paper is useful for small, delicate models.

You can even use pages from an old magazine, bus tickets or any small piece of paper.

Newspaper is handy for big models.

Writing paper folds well and is strong.

Silver and gold foil paper looks good.

Very thin cardboard is extra strong but harder to fold.

You could paint your own paper.

Symbols

Sometimes symbols are used to help you follow each step. These are the main ones:

Turn the paper over.

Turn the paper around.

Fold and then unfold the paper to make a crease.

2

To make a square

Top edge · Make sure these edges meet. · Bottom corner

A lot of origami models start with a square. Make a square from an oblong as above.

Fold the bottom corner up to the top edge to make a triangle.

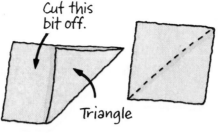

Cut this bit off. · Triangle

Cut along the side of the triangle you just made. Open out the paper to see your square.

Folding tips

You will learn lots of different folds through the book. The difficult ones are listed on page 32. The picture opposite shows you how to fold neatly. Below it are three good tips to remember.

‑ ‑ ‑ Valley fold.

‑ · ‑ Mountain fold.

This is a valley fold.

This is a mountain fold.

Hold the corners together. · Press down in the middle first. · Smooth to the side.

1. Always fold neatly, making sure the corners and edges meet. It is easier to be accurate if you fold away from you.

2. Work on a hard surface and press firmly along each fold.

3. Check the picture after every step to see if your paper looks the same.

TRICKY

Some folds are hard the first time you try them. Watch out for the 'tricky' warnings which mark the most difficult bits. If you get stuck fold something else and then try again later.

Tip

Small origami models often look best, but big ones are easier to fold. Start a new model with a big square. When you can fold it easily, use a small one.

To find the middle of a square

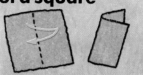

Fold the paper in half from side to side. Then unfold it.

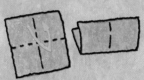

Then fold it in half from top to bottom and unfold it.

The middle is where the creases meet. · The middle

To find the middle of an edge

Pinch here.

Fold the corners together and pinch in the middle. Unfold it.

This is the middle.

The pinch mark is the middle.

3

Quick and easy boxes

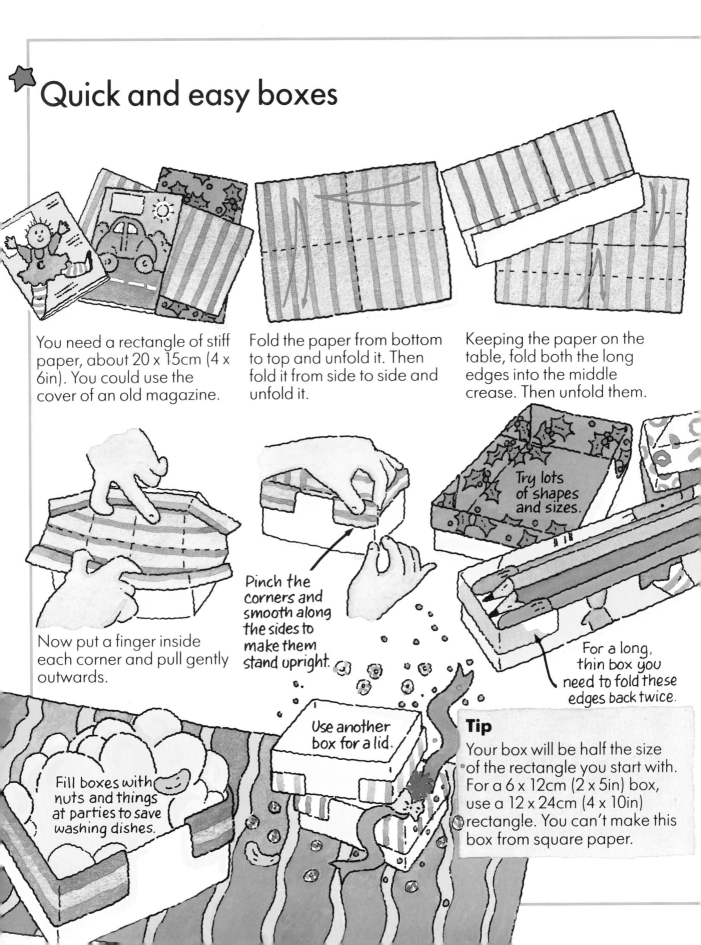

You need a rectangle of stiff paper, about 20 x 15cm (4 x 6in). You could use the cover of an old magazine.

Fold the paper from bottom to top and unfold it. Then fold it from side to side and unfold it.

Keeping the paper on the table, fold both the long edges into the middle crease. Then unfold them.

Now put a finger inside each corner and pull gently outwards.

Pinch the corners and smooth along the sides to make them stand upright.

Try lots of shapes and sizes.

For a long, thin box you need to fold these edges back twice.

Fill boxes with nuts and things at parties to save washing dishes.

Use another box for a lid.

Tip

Your box will be half the size of the rectangle you start with. For a 6 x 12cm (2 x 5in) box, use a 12 x 24cm (4 x 10in) rectangle. You can't make this box from square paper.

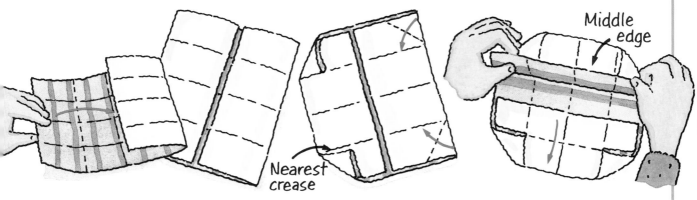

Middle edge

Fold both the short edges into the middle crease and leave them there.

Nearest crease

Fold in all the corners so that they meet the nearest crease, as shown here.

Fold back the edges in the middle so that they cover the corners.

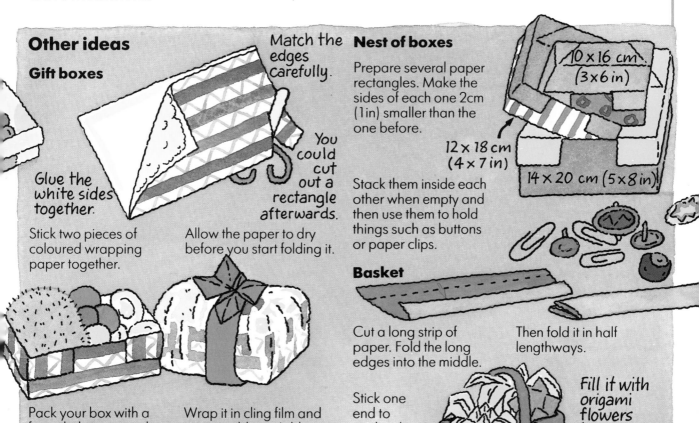

Other ideas

Gift boxes

Match the edges carefully.

Glue the white sides together.

Stick two pieces of coloured wrapping paper together.

You could cut out a rectangle afterwards.

Allow the paper to dry before you start folding it.

Pack your box with a face cloth, soap and bath pearls. Or fill it with sweets or nuts.

Wrap it in cling film and tie on a ribbon. Add a paper flower for decoration (see page 28).

Nest of boxes

Prepare several paper rectangles. Make the sides of each one 2cm (1in) smaller than the one before.

10 x 16 cm (3 x 6 in)

12 x 18 cm (4 x 7 in)

14 x 20 cm (5 x 8 in)

Stack them inside each other when empty and then use them to hold things such as buttons or paper clips.

Basket

Cut a long strip of paper. Fold the long edges into the middle.

Then fold it in half lengthways.

Stick one end to each side of a box.

Fill it with origami flowers (see page 28).

5

Party hats

To make hats that fit you need large squares. Wrapping paper is good. Or use newspaper and paint one side.

Pill box hat

Take a 40cm (12in) square of paper and label the corners in red and blue pen on both sides, as shown.

With the white side up, fold the blue corners together.

These edges line up.

Fold one red corner across to the opposite side so that the top and bottom edges line up.

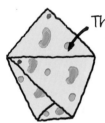

These edges meet.

This is the other side.

Stick a gift bow to the front and tuck a feather in the back.

Fold the other red corner across in the same way. Check that the edges meet.

Fold the top blue corner up over the edges. Turn the paper over and do the same again.

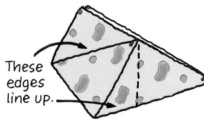

Other ideas
Bird mask

Leave the last corner, on the side with no folds, pointing down to make the beak. Paint it yellow.

Cut out nostrils so you can see through the holes.

Tape some feathers to the top for plumage.

Draw on big eyes.

Clown hat

Make a crepe paper fringe for the hair.

Stick a paper flower on the front.

To make the fringe

Use a strip of crepe paper about 15 x 30cm (6 x 12in). Make lots of cuts along one edge.

Glue the other edge inside the rim of your hat. Remember to leave a space for your face.

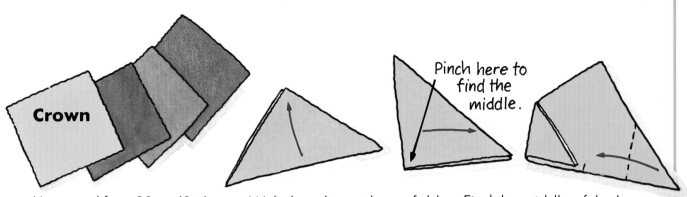

Crown

You need four 20cm (8in) squares of paper. Take one square and turn it so that one corner is towards you.

With the white side up, fold the bottom corner to the top corner.

Pinch here to find the middle.

Find the middle of the long edge by folding it in half. Then fold the side corners into the middle.

Fold all your squares in the same way. Then stand them in a square with the corners pointing inwards, ready to join together.

Make these folds meet.

To link them together slot each corner inside the one next to it, making sure that the folds meet.

Other ideas

Crown of jewels

Stick on gum drops or brightly-coloured buttons as jewels.

Or crumple up tinfoil and cover it with transparent, coloured wrappers.

Rich gold crown

Use paper that is coloured on both sides. Stick gold doilies to one side. Trim off any overlapping bits. Fold each square with the doily side down.

Bend the inner points into the centre and tape them together.

You could turn down the top corner to make a white diamond pattern.

Use more squares to make a bigger crown.

Add some tape to make the corners stronger.

Stick a jewel in the middle.

Bend these two first.

Flutter butterfly

This butterfly is very easy to fold and it flutters through the air when you throw it

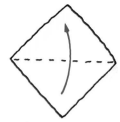

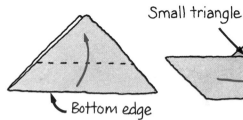

Small triangle

Bottom edge

Use a square of shiny paper for the best effect. Or paint on your own splatter design, as shown below.

Turn the paper so that one corner is towards you, white side up. Then fold the bottom corner to the top.

Fold up the bottom edge, leaving a small triangle peeping out at the top.

Fold the paper in half from side to side. Make sure all the edges meet.

Fold the top layer only here.

These are the wings.

It tumbles...

Fold back the top layer along the dotted line marked in the picture.

Turn the paper over and fold the other side in exactly the same way.

Make the wings stick out to the side. Hold the butterfly beneath them and throw it gently forwards.

... over

... and

... over.

To paint a splatter design

Make sure you have some newspaper underneath.

Fold the square in half diagonally. Then unfold it.

Splash some paint on one half of the paper only.

Start folding with the crease vertical like this.

Fold it in half and press down hard.

Unfold the paper and leave it to dry.

Space spinner

You need eight small squares of coloured paper. Use fluorescent or shiny paper for a really bright effect.

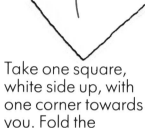

Take one square, white side up, with one corner towards you. Fold the bottom corner to the top corner.

Top corners

Right corner

Fold the right corner up to the top corners to make a small triangle.

Small triangle

Fold all the other squares in exactly the same way. Then join them together as shown below.

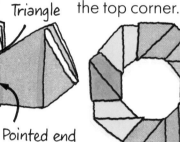

Push here to open the triangle.

Triangle

Pointed end

Slot the pointed end of each piece of paper inside the small triangle of the next one.

Keep joining them until you have a complete circle. Then turn the space spinner over.

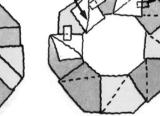

Fold the top one only.

Add tape to secure.

Fold back the top flap on each section so that it sticks up in the air.

Throw it flat, like a frisbee, to make it spin through the air.

Draw on windows with aliens peeping out.

Paint on landing lights with fluorescent pen.

9

⭐ Viking ship and snapping dragon

Both these models use the same folds to begin with. Start by doing the steps below.

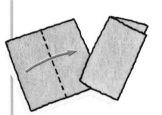 

Use a square of strong paper such as writing paper or brown wrapping paper. Fold it in half from side to side.

Fold the right edge back to meet the folded edge.

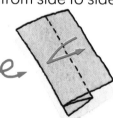 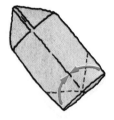

Turn the paper over. Fold the right edge back to the folded edge. Then unfold it.

Fold all the corners into the middle crease.

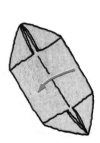 

Fold the right edge back to the folded edge again. Now you can make the viking ship or the snapping dragon.

10

Viking ship

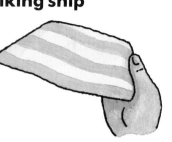

Hold the paper as shown here. Put your fingers inside and your thumb ½cm (¼in) from the top of the side fold.

With your other hand, push the corner over your thumbnail. Squash it down flat.

Fold the other corner in the same way.

Add a coin to balance it.

Turn the boat over and float it. It will sail best with something inside.

To make the mast and sail

Press some playdough in the bottom of the boat. Stick a drinking straw into it for the mast.

Snapping dragon

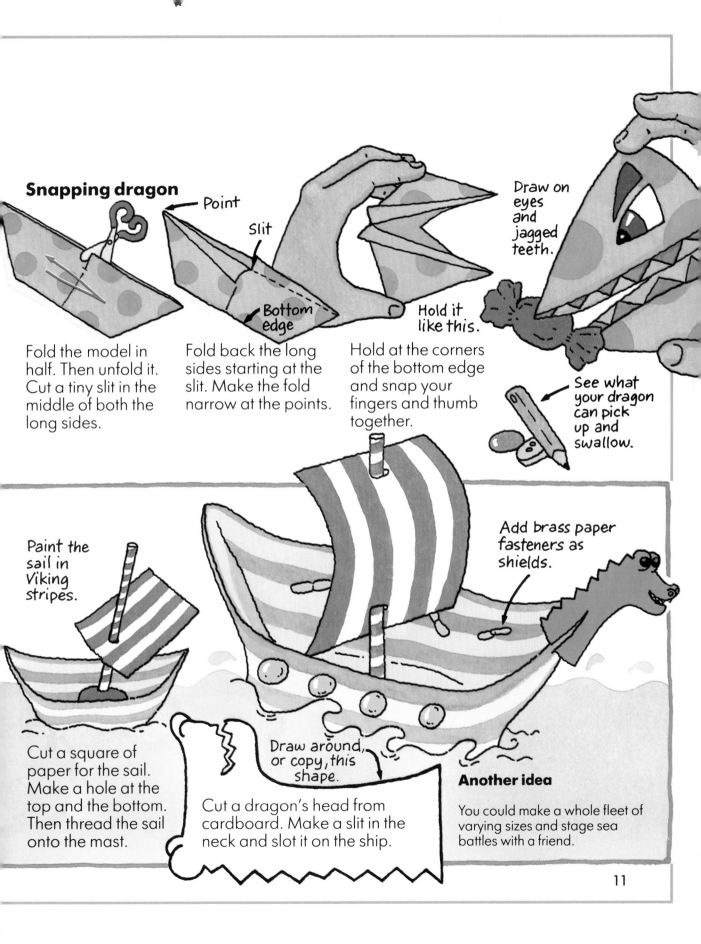

Point

Slit

Bottom edge

Fold the model in half. Then unfold it. Cut a tiny slit in the middle of both the long sides.

Fold back the long sides starting at the slit. Make the fold narrow at the points.

Hold it like this.

Hold at the corners of the bottom edge and snap your fingers and thumb together.

Draw on eyes and jagged teeth.

See what your dragon can pick up and swallow.

Paint the sail in Viking stripes.

Add brass paper fasteners as shields.

Cut a square of paper for the sail. Make a hole at the top and the bottom. Then thread the sail onto the mast.

Draw around, or copy, this shape.

Cut a dragon's head from cardboard. Make a slit in the neck and slot it on the ship.

Another idea

You could make a whole fleet of varying sizes and stage sea battles with a friend.

11

⭐Big bang

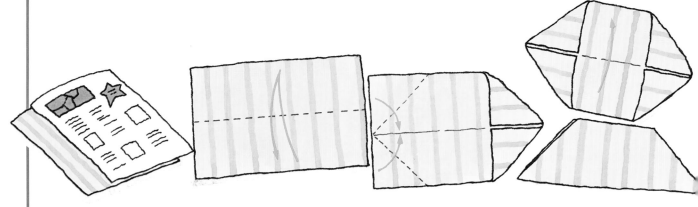

Take a large rectangle of thin paper. A sheet of newspaper or thin brown wrapping paper makes a good loud noise.

Fold the longest sides of the paper together. Then unfold them.

Fold down each corner, matching one side with the middle crease.

Fold the paper in half along the middle crease.

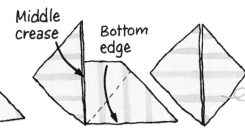

Middle crease

Bottom edge

Fold the paper in half again from side to side. Then unfold it.

Fold up the bottom corners so that the bottom edge meets the middle crease. Turn the paper over.

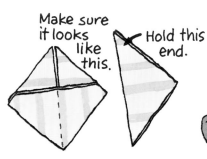

Make sure it looks like this.

Hold this end.

Have this edge towards you.

Fold it in half from side to side. Pick up the banger and hold it firmly at the open end.

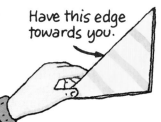

Make sure the long edge is towards you. Then put your hand in the air and bring it down sharply. The paper will open with a bang.

Other ideas

Try a 'quick on the draw' contest. See who can make the first bang after a count of three.

Or stand back to back with a friend, walk five paces away from each other, then see who can turn and draw first. Try a banger in each hand for double-barrelled draws.

12

Customize your banger

Try making bigger and smaller bangers. Each size makes a different noise.

Paint on different words and designs.

Stick on silver lightning flashes.

Write on noisy words.

Add glitter and sequins.

You could draw on clouds.

Snowstorm

Tear up lots of small pieces of paper and tuck them inside the fold. When the banger snaps open the "snow" will scatter all over your victim.

Add stars.

Be prepared to clear up afterwards.

ZAP!

ZOOM

CRACK!

BANG!

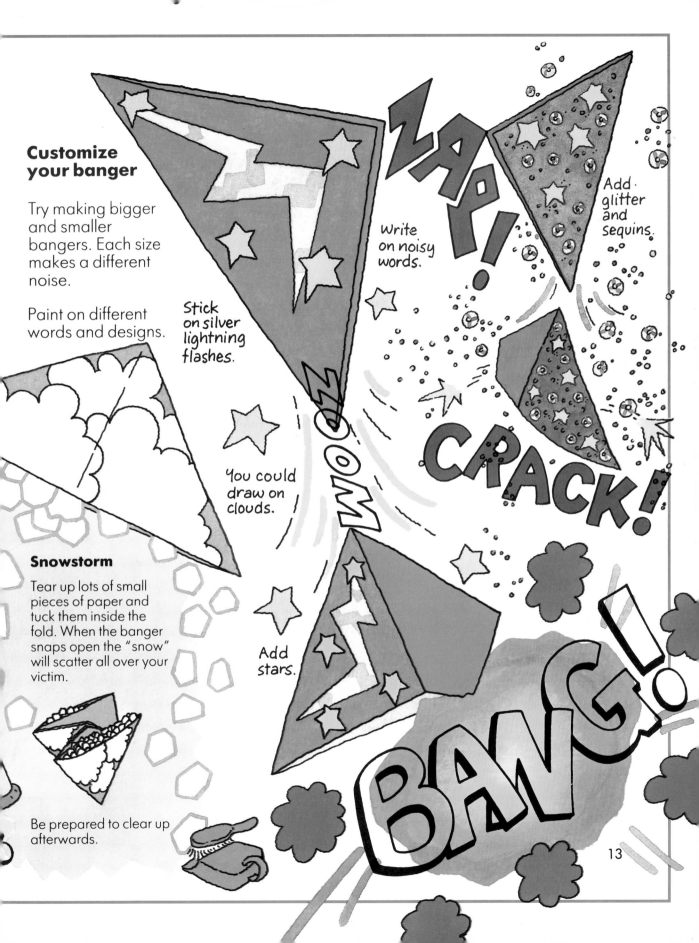

13

Fearsome fangs

Use a rectangle of paper twice as long as it is wide, for example, 8 x 16cm (3 x 6 in). Colour one side bright red for the lips.

Leave the other side white for the fangs. Label the corners green and blue on both sides as shown in the first picture.

Fold this edge.

With the white side up, fold the paper in half from side to side. Unfold it.

Fold it in half from top to bottom and then unfold it again.

Fold the green corners and the blue corners into the middle crease.

Fold the left edge into the middle again, to cover the green corners.

crease

These are the fangs.

Peep at the other side to check the fangs are long enough.

Check that your paper looks like the first picture above, then fold in again along the crease.

Fold the fangs out to the side so that they stick out over the edge.

Fold the right side into the middle so that the red lips meet and the white fangs stick out.

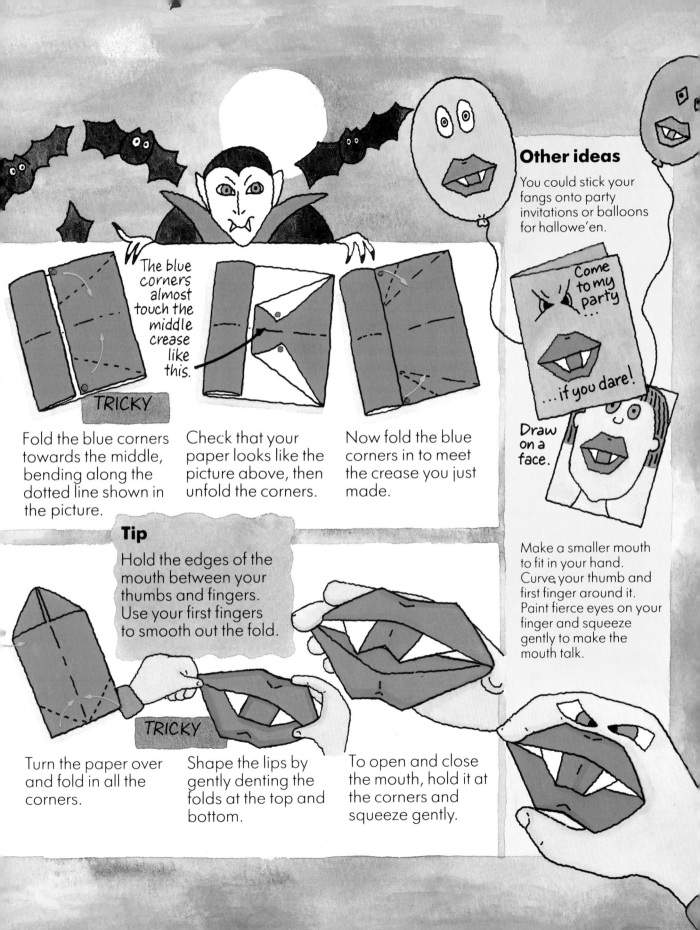

The blue corners almost touch the middle crease like this.

TRICKY

Fold the blue corners towards the middle, bending along the dotted line shown in the picture.

Check that your paper looks like the picture above, then unfold the corners.

Now fold the blue corners in to meet the crease you just made.

Other ideas

You could stick your fangs onto party invitations or balloons for hallowe'en.

Come to my party...

...if you dare!

Draw on a face.

Make a smaller mouth to fit in your hand. Curve your thumb and first finger around it. Paint fierce eyes on your finger and squeeze gently to make the mouth talk.

Tip

Hold the edges of the mouth between your thumbs and fingers. Use your first fingers to smooth out the fold.

TRICKY

Turn the paper over and fold in all the corners.

Shape the lips by gently denting the folds at the top and bottom.

To open and close the mouth, hold it at the corners and squeeze gently.

⭐⭐ Jumping frog

Take a rectangle of strong paper or very thin cardboard. A good size to start with is 10 x 15cm (6 x 4in). Label the corners red and blue as shown.

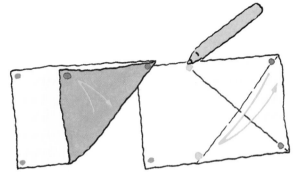

With the wrong side up, fold up one of the blue corners as if to make a square. Then unfold it.

Make sure the middle pops up.

Smaller frogs jump higher.

Fold the other blue corner in the same way. Then unfold it. Mark the ends of the new creases yellow on both sides.

Double legs are more springy.

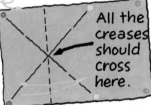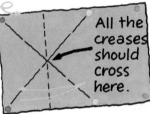

All the creases should cross here.

Turn the paper over. Fold the blue corners to the yellow marks. Then unfold them.

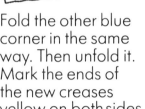

Put a finger at each end of that last crease and push gently inwards.

If your creases are firmly made, the middle will pop up, bringing the blue corners towards the yellow marks.

Make a high jump

Use coins and a thin strip of cardboard for the bar.

Add two more coins each time your frog clears the bar.

Here are some tips to make your frog jump higher:

Bend the front and back legs back a second time.

Or use springy cardboard, like a birthday card.

Or make a tiny frog. Smaller ones jump higher.

Bend the front legs like this

Bend the back legs like this.

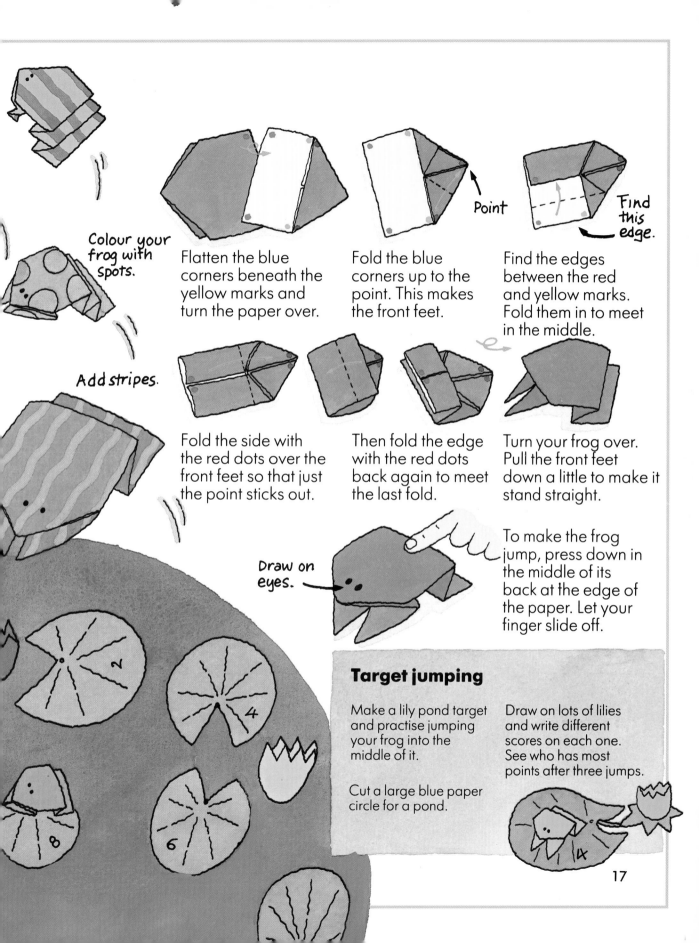

Colour your frog with spots.

Add stripes.

Flatten the blue corners beneath the yellow marks and turn the paper over.

Fold the blue corners up to the point. This makes the front feet.

Point

Find the edges between the red and yellow marks. Fold them in to meet in the middle.

Find this edge.

Fold the side with the red dots over the front feet so that just the point sticks out.

Then fold the edge with the red dots back again to meet the last fold.

Turn your frog over. Pull the front feet down a little to make it stand straight.

Draw on eyes.

To make the frog jump, press down in the middle of its back at the edge of the paper. Let your finger slide off.

Target jumping

Make a lily pond target and practise jumping your frog into the middle of it.

Cut a large blue paper circle for a pond.

Draw on lots of lilies and write different scores on each one. See who has most points after three jumps.

17

⭐ Bombs away

1. Use a square of strong paper. With the coloured side up, fold it in half from side to side. Then unfold it.

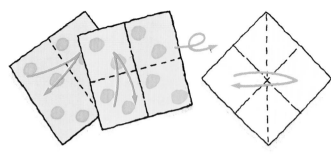

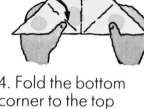

Hold below these creases.

2. Fold it in half from bottom to top. Unfold it and then turn the paper over.

3. Turn one corner towards you. Fold the side corners together and then unfold them.

4. Fold the bottom corner to the top corner. Pick up the paper and hold it at the bottom edge.

Leave this corner on the table.

Point

New Corner

Pocket

5. Push gently inwards. The top corners will move out and the side ones will move in.

6. Fold the front corner to one side and the back corner to the other side.

7. Press the paper flat on a table. Then fold the top two corners to the bottom point.

8. Fold the new corners into the middle. Look for the pockets this makes. You will need them later.

Push here to make the pocket open.

TRICKY

Point

Repeat on this side.

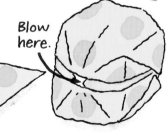

Blow here.

9. Find the two corners at the bottom point. Fold them to the edge of the pockets. Fold

them across the pockets. Unfold the last fold only and tuck the corners inside the pockets.

10. Turn the paper over and repeat from step 7.

11. Blow into the small hole at the bottom of the bomb to puff it up.

To charge the bomb pour some water into the hole. Throw it at a target, but only do it outdoors.

When it lands it will burst and soak whatever it hits.

White rabbit

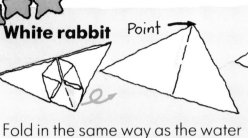

Point

Make an L-shape like this.

Bottom tips

Fold in the same way as the water bomb as far as step 9. Then use the other side to make the ears. Start with the point at the top.

Fold the side edges in to meet the middle crease.

Fold the bottom tips out to the side.

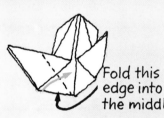

Blow here.

Fold this edge into the middle.

Paint it's ears and nose pink.

Add eyes and whiskers.

Fold all the layers at the bottom edge up to the middle crease.

Lift the ears up and hold them together. Pull down the bottom flaps.

Blow through the hole to inflate the rabbit's head.

Make a small rabbit from a 6cm (2½in) square to stick on the end of a pencil.

Tip

If the head wobbles glue it to the end of the pencil.

Other ideas

Use small waterbombs to make lots of different pencil puppets. Paint a different face on each plain side.

Robot

Use silver paper for the head (not kitchen foil because it tears).

Stick on a nose, eyes and mouth.

Use large pins for antennae.

Ghost

Use felt tips to draw a face.

Drape a thin white hanky over the pencil. Then stick the head on top.

Alien

Pull out the corners from the top pockets to make ears.

Finger puppets

Wizard

Use paper which has one white side. You need a 9cm (3in) square for the body and a 6cm (2in) square for the head.

white border

To make the body

Take the big square, white side up. Fold the sides together and unfold them.

Turn the paper over. Fold down ½cm (¼in) at the top.

Turn the paper over again and fold the top corners into the centre.

Fold the bottom edge behind, leaving a white border beneath the coloured triangles.

To make the head

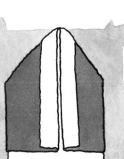

Turn it around and stand it up to see the finished body.

Use the small square. Have one corner towards you, white side up.

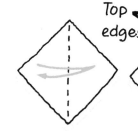

Top edges

Fold the side corners together. Then unfold them.

Make the corners meet here.

Fold the two edges at the top into the middle crease.

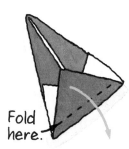

Fold here.

Fold the same corner back again from ½cm (¼in) above the last fold.

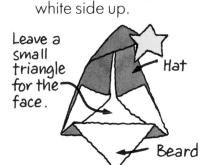

Leave a small triangle for the face.

Hat

Beard

Fold down the top of the hat and add a sticky gold star on the end of it.

Turn the paper over. Fold in the sides. Make them cross in the middle.

Tuck the right side into the left side. Push it in as far as the fold.

Fold here.

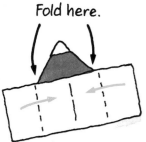

Hole for your finger.

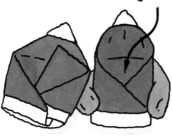

Turn the paper over to press the fold flat. Then fold the sides in.

Tuck the right side into the left side. Push it as far as the fold. This leaves a hole in the middle.

Find the corners in the middle. Fold them both out to meet the side edges.

This is the widest bit.

Now fold the bottom corner up along the widest bit of the paper.

Draw on a face.

Add glue to secure the head.

Balance the head on the body.

Stick star and moon shapes on the hat and cloak.

Then put it on your finger.

Other ideas

Use different coloured paper to make new puppets. Try changing the hat and cloak.

Green elf

Curl the hat forwards round a pencil. Roll the cloak back.

Wise old man

Stick the head on upside down for a very long beard.

Wise old man

Add cotton wool to his head and beard.

Santa Claus

Use Christmas wrapping paper. Tuck small gifts and rolled up paper into the top of his sack.

Santa Claus

Green elf

Sleepy head

Sleepy head

You could use just the head. Make it from a 9cm (3in) square. Use striped paper for the nightcap. Add cotton wool for a pom pom.

21

⭐ Jewellery

All the things on the next pages are made from the same base.
The blue box in the middle of this page shows how to make it.

To make a preliminary base

To make half a bead

You need two halves to
make a whole bead. First
make a preliminary base as
shown in the blue box. Then
continue like this:

Tip

Press down at the
bottom of the fold
first and smooth
upwards, making
sure the middle
creases meet.

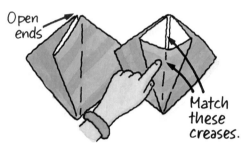

Open ends

Match these creases.

1. Turn the left flap so that it sticks up
in the air. Then squash fold it flat,
starting at the bottom.

Small flap

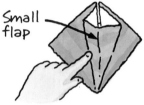

2. Turn the paper
over and repeat
step 1.

3. Fold the small
flap on the left over
to the right.

Big flap   Small flap

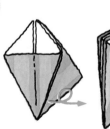

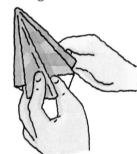

4. Make the big flap
on the left stand up
and then squash
fold it flat as before.

5. Turn the paper
over and repeat
steps 3 and 4.
When you finish,
there should be four
flaps on each side.

6. Fan out the flaps
in a circle to
complete the half
bead.

Take one square,
coloured side up.
Make two creases
by folding the
opposite corners
together.

Leave the paper
folded in half from
bottom to top and
hold it along the
fold, as shown.

Fold the flap in front
to the right and the
flap behind to the
left.

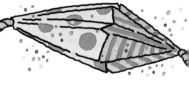

Make the centre folds meet.

Turn the paper over. Make two more creases by folding the paper in half from side to side and from bottom to top.

Gently bring your fingers together so that all the corners meet in the middle.

Flatten the paper to finish the base. Check there are two flaps on each side.

Slotting two halves together

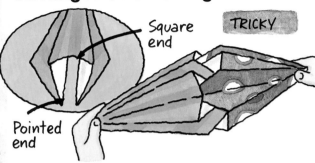

Square end

TRICKY

Pointed end

When you have made two halves, join them like this: slot the pointed ends of each half under the square ends of the other.

Dip the edges in glue and then glitter.

Make a large bead first, it's easier. Then see how small you can make your beads. Use them to make necklaces or earrings.

Add small waterbombs as round beads (see page 18).

Make a loop to go around your ear.

Tip

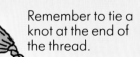

First fit the two halves together roughly. Then work your way around the bead, slotting one point in at a time.

To thread the beads

Use thin wire, such as fuse wire, to make a long needle. Make a loop at one end and tie on some thread.

Make sure your needle is longer than the bead.

Snip off each end of the bead to make a hole to thread through.

Remember to tie a knot at the end of the thread.

Flapping bird

The bird base is used as a starting point for many origami models. The flapping bird is one of them. Another famous one is the crane which is a symbol of good luck in Japan.

To make the bird base

1. Start with a preliminary base from page 22. Turn it so that the open ends are towards you.

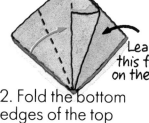

2. Fold the bottom edges of the top flaps only into the middle. Crease well. Then unfold them.

Leave this flap on the table.

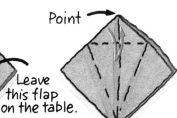

Point

3. Make a strong crease across the top by folding down the point. Then unfold it.

TRICKY

4. Lift up the top flap only at the corner nearest you. Put a finger on the others to keep them on the table.

5. Stretch it all the way over the point, bending at the crease you made in step 3. The sides

should fold inwards along the creases you made in step 2. Press it down flat.

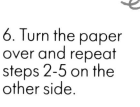

6. Turn the paper over and repeat steps 2-5 on the other side.

24

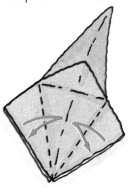

This is the finished bird base.

Hang more straws and birds from the other end.

Tip

Check that your mobile balances each time you add a new straw.

If one side is too heavy move the thread in the middle towards the heavy side.

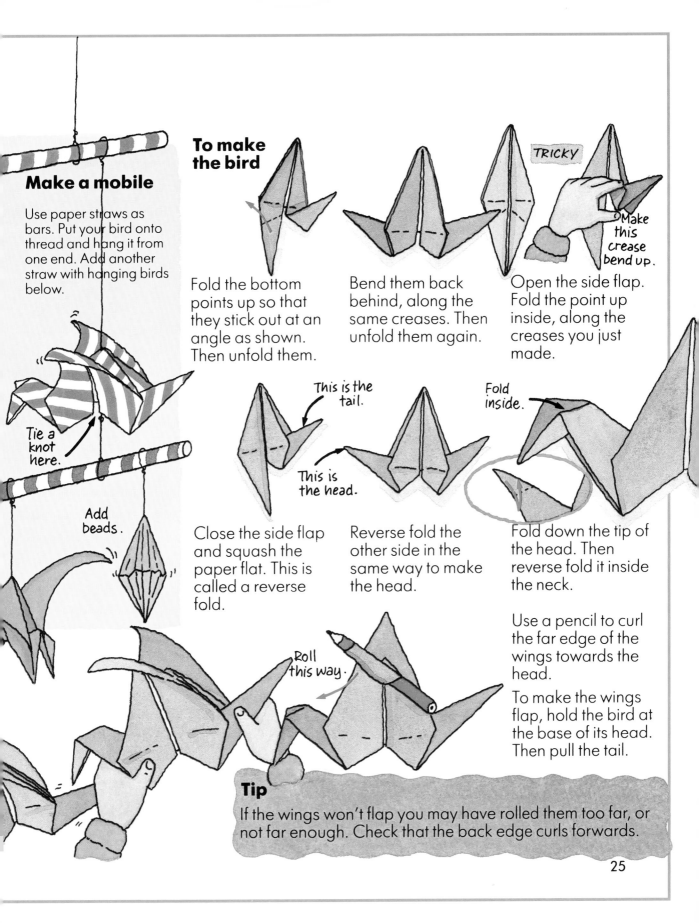

Make a mobile

Use paper straws as bars. Put your bird onto thread and hang it from one end. Add another straw with hanging birds below.

Tie a knot here.

Add beads.

To make the bird

TRICKY

Make this crease bend up.

Fold the bottom points up so that they stick out at an angle as shown. Then unfold them.

Bend them back behind, along the same creases. Then unfold them again.

Open the side flap. Fold the point up inside, along the creases you just made.

This is the tail.

This is the head.

Fold inside.

Close the side flap and squash the paper flat. This is called a reverse fold.

Reverse fold the other side in the same way to make the head.

Fold down the tip of the head. Then reverse fold it inside the neck.

Use a pencil to curl the far edge of the wings towards the head.

To make the wings flap, hold the bird at the base of its head. Then pull the tail.

Roll this way.

Tip

If the wings won't flap you may have rolled them too far, or not far enough. Check that the back edge curls forwards.

Star box

This box is also made from a preliminary base. You could use it as a jewellery box. Use wrapping paper or decorate your own paper before you start, as shown below.

To decorate the paper

Stick two sheets of wrapping paper together (see gift boxes on page 5). You could use gold paper for a really striking rim.

Or use plain coloured paper and paint a pattern on one side, starting in the middle.

Open ends

Bottom edges

Leave this flap on the table.

1. Start by making a preliminary base (see page 22). Turn the paper so that the open ends are towards you.

2. Fold the bottom edges of the top flaps only into the middle crease.

3. Turn the paper over and repeat step 2.

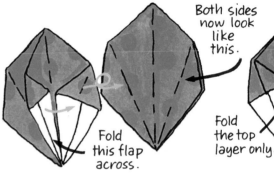

Both sides now look like this.

Fold this flap across.

Fold the top layer only.

6. Turn the paper over and repeat steps 4 and 5.

7. Fold the left flap over to the right. Turn the paper over and do the same on the other side.

8. Fold in the sides along the creases already there. Then turn the paper over.

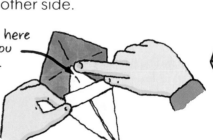
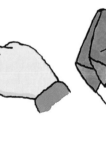

Leave these bits on the table.

Make the fold for step 12 here.

Hold here as you fold.

11. Fold the top flap only up to the cross where the two creases meet.

12. Fold up again, where the white side meets the coloured side.

13. Turn the left flap to the right and then repeat steps 11 and 12 on this side.

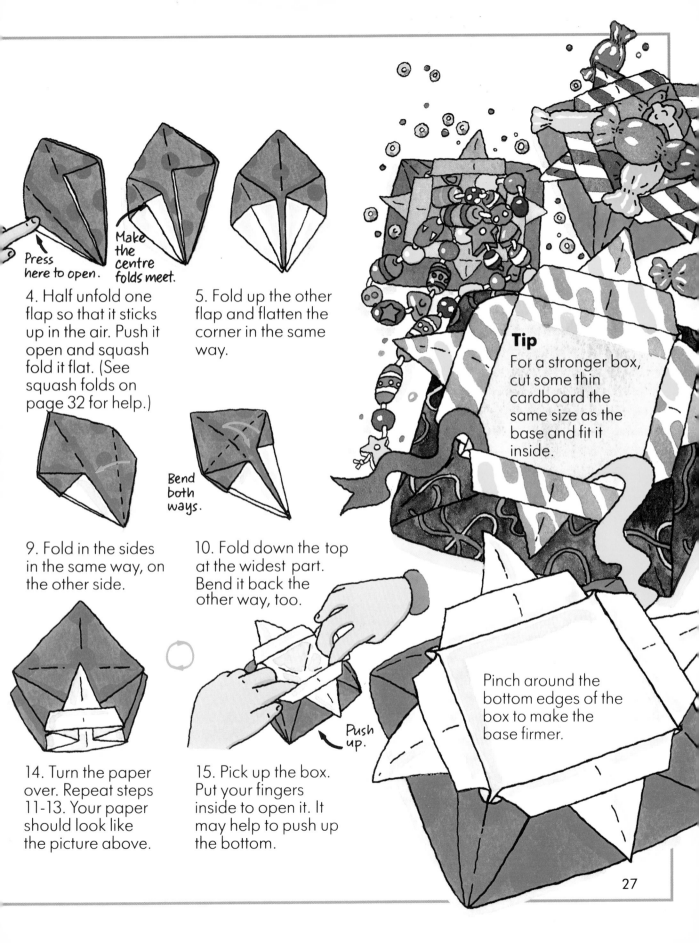

Press here to open.

Make the centre folds meet.

4. Half unfold one flap so that it sticks up in the air. Push it open and squash fold it flat. (See squash folds on page 32 for help.)

5. Fold up the other flap and flatten the corner in the same way.

Bend both ways.

9. Fold in the sides in the same way, on the other side.

10. Fold down the top at the widest part. Bend it back the other way, too.

Push up.

Tip

For a stronger box, cut some thin cardboard the same size as the base and fit it inside.

Pinch around the bottom edges of the box to make the base firmer.

14. Turn the paper over. Repeat steps 11-13. Your paper should look like the picture above.

15. Pick up the box. Put your fingers inside to open it. It may help to push up the bottom.

Lily

This is the most difficult model in the book but you can make it using folds you have learned earlier. Use a square of two-coloured paper for the best effect. First fold it into a half bead (see page 22) then continue like this:

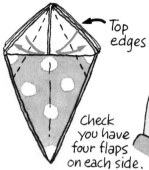

Top edges

Check you have four flaps on each side.

Lift here.

1. With the open ends to the top, fold the top edges of the top flap only into the centre. Then unfold them.

2. Hold the paper down firmly at the top and bottom as shown. Then lift up the top flap.

3. Pull the flap towards you, folding the sides into the middle. They will bend along the creases you made in step 1.

Check all the small triangles are pointing up.

Do the same on the other side too.

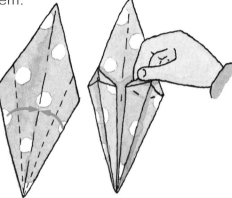

When you have finished your paper should look like this.

7. Turn the left flap over to the right. Then turn the paper over and do the same on the other side.

8. Fold the bottom sides into the middle as shown.

9. Repeat step 8 on the other three sides.

10. Use a pencil to curl each petal. Start on the top flap and then do the same on the three other sides.

Tip

Roll the first petal on the table. Turn the paper over and rest it gently on the table as you roll the second. You will need to open the flower slightly to find the two side petals.

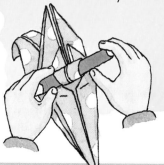

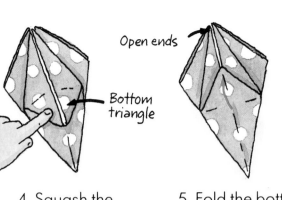

Open ends

Bottom triangle

When you have finished your paper should look like this.

How to repeat a step on three sides

Turn the paper over and repeat for the first time.

4. Squash the bottom triangle down flat. This is the petal fold (see page 32 for help).

5. Fold the bottom triangle up towards the open ends.

6. Now repeat steps 1-5 on the three other sides. See how to do this on the right.

Turn the large flap on the left over to the right and repeat for the second time.

Bunch of flowers

Use fat, bendy drinking straws for stems.

Tie lots of flowers in a bunch.

Large flap

Poke the end of the flower in to the straw.

Large flap

Turn the paper over. Then turn the large flap on the left over to the right and repeat for the third time.

Another idea
Tulip

Take a two-coloured square of paper. Fold all the corners into the middle to make a smaller square.

Use this square, folded side up, to make a waterbomb (see page 18). When you blow it up you will have two-coloured petals.

29

Stacking tree

To make the branches

Cut a large green square first. Now cut four more, making each one smaller than the one before.

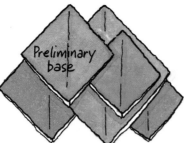

Preliminary base

Fold all the squares into preliminary bases (see page 22). Then continue like this for each one.

1. With the open end of the base towards you, fold up the top flap. Then unfold it.

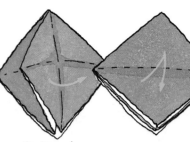

2. Do the same on the other three sides (see the tip on page 29 for help).

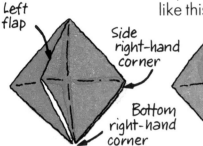

Left flap

Side right-hand corner

Bottom right-hand corner

3. Turn the left flap so that it sticks up in the air.

4. Take the bottom right-hand corner up to meet the side right-hand corner.

Small triangle   Shelf

5. Hold the corners firmly together. Then flatten the small triangle below to make a little shelf.

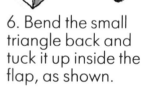

TRICKY

6. Bend the small triangle back and tuck it up inside the flap, as shown.

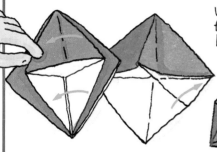

7. Lift the right flap up so the shelf goes over to the left. Then repeat steps 4-6 on the next flap.

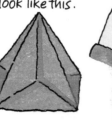

When you have finished it should look like this.

8. Fold the two flaps on the other side in the same way. You will need to pick the paper up.

Tip

The last little triangle may be tricky to fold inside. Try opening up the paper a little and pushing it in with a finger.

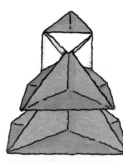

9. When all the branches are folded, slot one on top of the other.

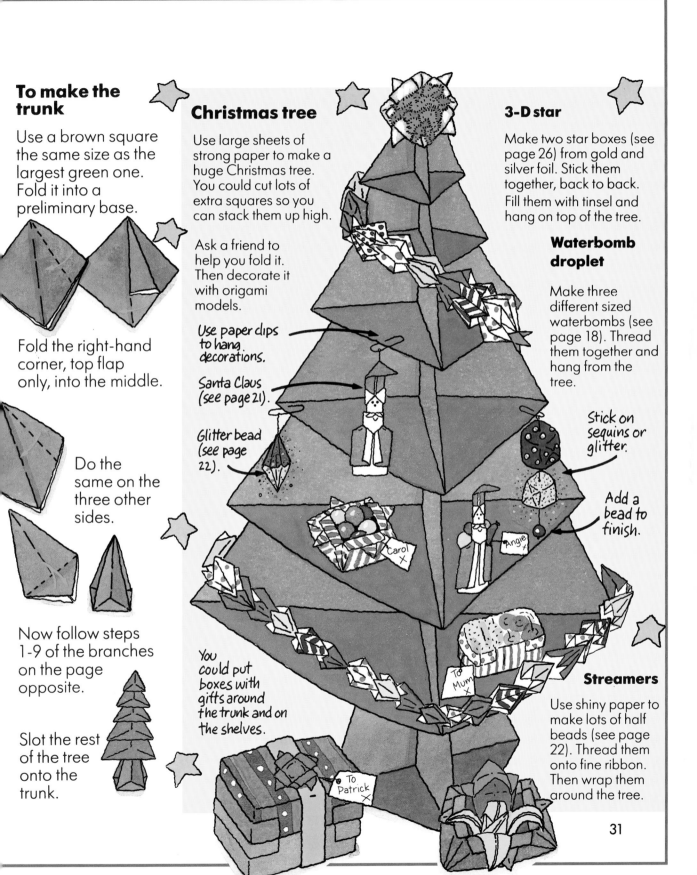

To make the trunk

Use a brown square the same size as the largest green one. Fold it into a preliminary base.

Fold the right-hand corner, top flap only, into the middle.

Do the same on the three other sides.

Now follow steps 1-9 of the branches on the page opposite.

Slot the rest of the tree onto the trunk.

Christmas tree

Use large sheets of strong paper to make a huge Christmas tree. You could cut lots of extra squares so you can stack them up high.

Ask a friend to help you fold it. Then decorate it with origami models.

Use paper clips to hang decorations.

Santa Claus (see page 21).

Glitter bead (see page 22).

You could put boxes with gifts around the trunk and on the shelves.

3-D star

Make two star boxes (see page 26) from gold and silver foil. Stick them together, back to back. Fill them with tinsel and hang on top of the tree.

Waterbomb droplet

Make three different sized waterbombs (see page 18). Thread them together and hang from the tree.

Stick on sequins or glitter.

Add a bead to finish.

Streamers

Use shiny paper to make lots of half beads (see page 22). Thread them onto fine ribbon. Then wrap them around the tree.

31

Tricky folds

Some folds are used over and over again in lots of different origami models, so it is useful to remember how to do them. Here are three tricky folds which you have learned in this book and may find useful for other models.

The origami models in this book that are not traditional were designed by Sarah Goodall (Fearsome fangs); Nick Robinson (Crown); Susanna Kricskovics (Finger puppets); Makoto Yamaguchi (Stacking tree and tulip).

If you would like to find out more about origami and learn how to make more models, you could contact Dave Brill at the British Origami Society, 253 Park Lane, Poynton, Stockport SK12 1RH.

Reverse fold

Crease

Push inside.

First make a strong crease where shown by bending the paper both ways.

Then open the paper out above the crease you just made.

Finally, push the paper above the crease down, so that it folds inside the rest of the paper.

Squash fold

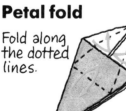

Lift up.

Tap here to open.

Match these folds.

First lift up the corner that is going to be squashed flat.

Then open the corner by pressing along the fold.

Finally press it flat, starting at the bottom. Keep the two centre folds together.

Petal fold

Hold the ends down on the table.

Fold along the dotted lines.

Edge of the top layer

These are the creases you made earlier.

First make all the preparation creases. Press down firmly to make them really strong.

Then lift up the edge of the top layer. Hold the other layers firmly on the table.

Finally, stretch the edge of the top layer down towards you. The paper will fold along the creases you made earlier.